HEREFORD

TRAVEL GUIDE

2024

EXPLORING THE HEART OF ENGLAND'S
COUNTRYSIDE

JOEL BURKE

Copyright © 2024, Joel Burke

All rights reserved.

No part of this publication may be reproduced, distributed, or transmitted in any form or by any means, including photocopying, recording, or other electronic or mechanical methods, without the prior written permission of the publisher, except in the case of brief quotations embodied in critical reviews and certain other noncommercial uses permitted by copyright law.

TABLE OF CONTENTS

Introduction	3
Chapter 1: Getting to Hereford	8
Chapter 2: Hereford's Delightful Foods	18
Chapter 3: Hereford's Countryside Escapes	27
Chapter 4: Art and Culture in Hereford	33
Chapter 5: Shopping in Hereford	39
Chapter 6: Accommodations in Hereford	45
Chapter 7: Events and Festivals	55
Chapter 8: Practical Information	62
Chapter 9: Exploring Beyond Hereford	70
Conclusion	78

Introduction

Welcome to Hereford, a welcoming city that beckons you to stroll through its meandering streets and discover a centuries-spanning past. You'll be engrossed in a lot of experiences that skillfully blend the ancient and the new, the traditional and the modern, from the minute you step foot on this holy land.

The friendliness of Hereford's citizens is just as evident as the city's architectural treasures and scenic attractions. Discovering the vibrant markets, sampling regional specialties in a centuries-old tavern, or stopping to take in the exquisite features of Hereford Cathedral will all make you feel a part of a community that is proud to share its history.

A Summary of the Historical Significance of Hereford

Hereford's character has been influenced by several layers of history, which must be explored to be fully appreciated. The city's beginnings may be found in the Saxon period, when a hamlet appeared on the Wye River's banks. The name's origin, which combines the words "here" (for army or troops) and "ford" (for river crossing), alludes to the location's strategic significance.

Hereford Cathedral was built due to a significant chapter that began with the Norman Conquest in the eleventh century. The throbbing center of the city is this architectural wonder, a monument to the influences of Norman, Gothic, and Romanesque architecture. The Mappa Mundi, a medieval map that provides a vivid image of the medieval worldview, is housed inside its hallowed walls.

The historical importance of Hereford is not limited to its cathedral; it is also evident in its Tudor and medieval architecture, historical locations, and cultural icons. Every city area has a backstory that begs to be discovered to piece together a rich and diverse history.

What to Expect in this Travel Handbook

This detailed Hereford travel guide emerges as your travel companion in the pages that follow. It has been designed to serve as your entry point to the wide range of attractions in the city, giving advice and suggestions to make your visit unforgettable.

Delicious Foods: Savor the tastes of Hereford in both neighborhood restaurants and historic pubs, which provide filling meals. Explore the heart of Hereford's culinary culture, which combines regional ingredients with time-honored classics.

Historical Journey: Explore the many eras of Hereford's past, from the Saxon origins of the city to the stunning architecture of the cathedral. Discover the stories woven into the structure and significance of each building as you visit the city's historic landmarks.

Countryside Escapes: Go beyond the city's boundaries to the peaceful sanctuaries around

Hereford. Take part in outdoor activities, such as cycling or nature hikes, and lose yourself in the unspoiled beauty that characterizes the English countryside.

Culture and Art: Explore galleries, museums, and performance spaces to immerse yourself in Hereford's thriving cultural scene. Engage with the local community of artists and craftspeople to learn about the vibrant creative culture of Hereford.

Shopping: Explore the quaint alleys with their mix of high-street stores, boutiques, and lively markets. Discover distinctive mementos and regional handicrafts that perfectly capture Hereford's spirit.

Accommodations: A variety of lodging options are available to suit a range of tastes and price ranges. Hereford has lodging alternatives to accommodate every kind of tourist, whether they like the contemporary hotel or the ancient beauty of a bed and breakfast.

Festivals and Events: Become fully immersed in the culture of the area by going to festivals and yearly events. Learn about the customs and festivals that unite the community all year.

Useful Details: Prepare yourself for any eventuality by learning about local traditions, emergency contacts, and transport choices. With these tips, you can make sure your trip to Hereford is easy and pleasurable.

Exploring Beyond Hereford: Learn about suggested routes for seeing the countryside and day trip choices to neighboring destinations. Continue your journey to nearby towns and villages, each with a distinct charm of its own.

This guide will take you on a deep dive into Hereford's spirit as you flip the pages. Allow the tales to unravel, the tastes to entice, and the scenery to delight you. Hereford is waiting to be discovered, enjoyed, and experienced.

Chapter 1: Getting to Hereford

A seamless and pleasurable travel experience is ensured by carefully considering your transportation choices before departing for Hereford, a charming city tucked away in the heart of England. To ensure a smooth arrival in Hereford, this comprehensive reference gives insightful information on several transportation options, indicates the closest airports and rail stations, and includes thorough driving instructions and parking information.

Transportation Options and Diverse Choices for Every Traveler

Hereford draws tourists from all over the world with its enthralling scenery and rich history. The city provides a variety of transportation choices to meet the various demands of visitors. Hereford offers a variety of travel options, including air travel for convenience, rail travel for scenic appeal, and driving for flexibility.

Air Travel

If you choose to travel by air, Hereford is well-connected to several major airports, making access quick and pleasant. Bristol Airport (BRS) and Birmingham Airport (BHX) are the two main airports servicing the area.

- ★ **Birmingham Airport (BHX):** The main international hub, Birmingham Airport, is located around 70 miles northeast of Hereford and has great connections. From the airport, visitors may easily take a direct rail or bus, or hire a vehicle for a picturesque drive through the English countryside to get to Hereford.

- ★ **Bristol Airport (BRS):** Bristol Airport is another convenient place to fly, situated around 120 miles southwest of Hereford. To get to Hereford from Bristol, travelers may use a train, bus, or automobile, taking in the ever-changing scenery as they go.

Rail Trips

Still, a popular option for those looking for a leisurely and pleasing trip to Hereford is taking the train. The Hereford Railway Station acts as a vital center for several train services, providing excellent rail connections around the city. Hereford has direct rail connections to major cities such as Manchester, Birmingham, and London.

★ **London to Hereford:** The direct train travels quickly and comfortably between London, Paddington, and Hereford, offering beautiful vistas of the English countryside as you go. For those coming from the capital, the train is a handy choice since the trip takes around three hours.

★ **Birmingham to Hereford**: Direct trains from Birmingham to Hereford provide hassle-free travel that takes around one and a half hours. The train service offers a cozy, charming path so that travelers may unwind.

Driving (Exploring at Your Own Pace)

Road access to Hereford is convenient for those who value the freedom and independence that come with driving. The region's road system is kept up properly, making for a comfortable and pleasurable ride. Important connections that link Hereford to important cities and highways include the M5 and M50 motorways.

Closest Train Stations and Airports. (Entry Points to Hereford)

It is essential to know the locations of rail stations and airports to organize an easy trip to Hereford. The information about the closest rail stations and airports is as follows:

1. Airports

★ **Airport Birmingham (BHX):** The closest major international airport is

Birmingham Airport, which is located around 70 miles northeast of Hereford. It is a handy entry point for guests coming by plane, with first-rate transit connections.

★ **Airport Bristol (BRS):** Bristol Airport is another convenient airport, located around 120 miles southwest of Hereford. The airport is well-connected to Hereford by several different transit options and provides a variety of services.

2. Train Stations

★ **Hereford Railway Station**: Hereford Train Station links Hereford to major cities nationwide and serves as the city's main train hub. Due to its strategic location, the station offers quick access to both the city's heart and its environs.

★ **Leominster Railway Station:** Another easily accessible alternative for passengers is Leominster Railway Station, which is located around 12 miles north of Hereford. Regular train services are available at the station, which links Hereford to the larger rail system.

How to Drive and Where to Park: Getting Around the Roadways

If you want to drive yourself around Hereford's scenic landscapes, you'll need accurate driving instructions and parking information to ensure a stress-free trip. Here are detailed directions to help you get to Hereford and ensure a seamless arrival:

From Birmingham Airport (BHX):

★ **By Car:** After leaving the airport, take the M42 freeway and join the M5 heading south. Proceed on the M5 until you get to junction 7, then get onto the M50 in the direction of Ross-on-Wye and Hereford. When you get closer to Hereford, follow the signs.

★ **By Train:** Take a direct train to Hereford Railway Station from Birmingham New Street. After arriving, local transportation or taxis make it simple to go to the city center.

★ **Packing**: Hereford has a range of parking options, including on-street parking and multi-story parking lots. In addition to pay-and-display parking alternatives, tourists may park conveniently in designated zones inside the city center.

From Bristol Airport (BRS)

★ **By Car**: Take the A38 out of the airport and turn right to join the M5 heading north. Proceed on the M5 until you get to junction 8, then turn left onto the M50 to Ross-on-Wye and Hereford. When you get closer to Hereford, follow the signs.

★ **By Train:** Travel to Hereford Railway Station from Bristol Temple Meads via rail. Taxis and other local transportation make it simple to get to the city center from the station.

★ *Parking:* Hereford has a variety of parking choices, including long- and short-term parking structures. For easy access to the core, visitors may take advantage of the Park and Ride facilities offered by the city.

From London (City Center):

★ **By Car:** Take the M4 motorway west and then the M48, which leads to Chepstow. After crossing the Severn Bridge, get onto the M49 and then turn onto the northbound M5. Take the M50 in the direction of Hereford and Ross-on-Wye at junction 8. When you get closer to Hereford, follow the signs.

★ **By Train:** Take a direct train to Hereford Railway Station from London Paddington. After arriving, local transportation or taxis make it simple to go to the city center.

★ **Parking:** There are many on-street and off-street parking alternatives available in Hereford's city center. Pay-and-display parking options are available for those who want hassle-free parking.

Parking in Hereford

★ **On-Street Parking:** There are time-limited on-street parking zones in the city center. Pay-and-display devices allow guests to pay for parking.

★ **Multi-Level Parking Garages:** Hereford has many multi-level parking lots, such as the parking lots of the Old Market and Maylord Shopping Center. For those who prefer to explore the city on foot, these facilities provide easy parking choices.

★ **Park & Ride:** For individuals who would rather leave their automobiles outside the city center, Hereford has Park & Ride services. This parking choice is easy and environmentally sustainable, with bus connections that are well-connected.

Whether you're traveling to Hereford by plane, rail, or automobile, these comprehensive travel resources include driving instructions, the closest airports and train stations, and extensive transit alternatives.

Chapter 2: Hereford's Delightful Foods

Let's explore Hereford's culinary highlights, the city's charming old pubs and restaurants, and the must-try regional foods and drinks that contribute to an incredibly memorable Hereford dining experience.

Highlights of Hereford's food

The food scene in Hereford is a dynamic blend of inventive cooking methods, regional ingredients, and classic British cuisine. The city is proud of its varied offers, which suit a variety of inclinations. Hereford provides a culinary experience that tantalizes the taste buds and fulfills the spirit, from charming tearooms selling exquisite pastries to fine dining venues exhibiting the finest of local products.

Excellent Dining Venues

Hereford offers an array of exquisite dining options that take the foodie experience to new levels. These restaurants often purchase their supplies locally, guaranteeing both freshness and a nod to the area's long history of agriculture. Expect well-designed dishes that emphasize the aromas of the surrounding countryside and the culinary prowess of Hereford's chefs.

- ★ **The Green Dragon:** Located in the center of Hereford, The Green Dragon is well-known for its dedication to sustainability and using products that are acquired locally. The meal honors the rich agricultural heritage of the area while celebrating contemporary British cuisine.

- ★ **Castle House Hotel:** The elegant dining experience at Castle House Hotel is set against the majestic backdrop of Hereford Castle. The restaurant's cuisine, which highlights the finest of seasonal ingredients, is a great tour across Herefordshire.

Quaint Tearooms and Cafés

Hereford's tearooms and cafés provide a pleasant escape for those looking for a more relaxed ambiance. Whether you're in the mood for a short coffee break or a leisurely afternoon tea, these places provide a lovely atmosphere for unwinding and enjoying delicious delicacies.

- ★ **Sensational Scones**: Hereford's tearooms are renowned for their delicious scones, which are often served with handmade jam and clotted cream. Both residents and tourists are drawn in by the welcoming mood created by the scent of freshly made pastries filling the air.

- ★ **The Herefordian Café:** Locals love The Herefordian Café, which is tucked away in a charming area of the city. Hereford's culinary legacy is captured in its cuisine of traditional British comfort food, paired with rustic charm.

Traditional Pubs and Local Eateries

A visit to Hereford's classic pubs and neighborhood restaurants would be incomplete without experiencing the hospitality and genuineness of these establishments. Not only do these locations provide satisfying meals, but they also function as community centers where residents and guests gather to experience the true spirit of Herefordshire.

1. The Black Lion: A Historic Haven for Pint and Pie

Entering the Black Lion feels like traveling through time. Charm and character abound in this ancient bar with its timbered façade and comfortable interior. The Black Lion is well-known for its wide assortment of regional ales and ciders, and it serves substantial pies—a staple of British pub fare—with its beverages.

> ★ **Signature Pies:** A variety of flavor-bursting trademark pies are

available on the pub's menu. The Black Lion takes pride in its dedication to utilizing locally sourced foods in everything it serves, from traditional steak and ale pies to creative vegetarian alternatives.

★ **Beers and Ciders in the Area:** The best ales and ciders from Herefordshire are proudly offered in a changing variety at the bar. In this old building, patrons may have a pint while taking in the warm atmosphere.

2. The Bookshop: A Blend of Literary and Culinary Pleasures

In Hereford's culinary scene, The Bookshop is a special find that combines a love of books with cuisine. This eccentric restaurant serves food inspired by great books and novels and is housed in a former bookstore.

★ **Literary-Inspired Dishes**: The Bookshop's menu includes items that are inspired by well-known literary works. Every meal, from the "Great Expectations" soup to the "To Kill a Mockingbird" fried chicken, is a lighthearted ode to the literary world.

★ **Cozy Reading Nooks:** The restaurant's book-lined shelves and comfortable reading corners capture the spirit of its literary history. The Bookshop offers a unique eating experience where patrons may indulge in sweet delicacies while losing themselves in a story.

Recommended Local Foods and Drinks: Hereford on a Plate

The agricultural background of the area is important to Hereford's culinary identity, and the rich tastes produced by the lush terrain are evident in the cuisine and drinks of the area. Hereford's culinary culture is best experienced by sampling its must-try items, which range from craft ciders to delicious meats.

1. Herefordshire Beef: A Cut Above the Rest

Herefordshire is known for its premium beef, so a trip to the area wouldn't be complete without indulging in a meal that highlights this specialty. The Hereford breed is recognized for producing soft, flavorful meat with its characteristic red and white characteristics.

- ★ **Beer pie with steak:** Savor a traditional steak and ale pie prepared with Herefordshire cattle that is sourced locally. The dish's tasty and cozy blend of flaky pastry, rich sauce, and delicate meat pieces perfectly captures the region's culinary brilliance.

- ★ **Beef Roast:** In local taverns and restaurants, traditional Sunday roasts made with Herefordshire beef are a popular option. The beef roast served with Yorkshire pudding, seasonal vegetables, and plenty of gravy is a filling and substantial meal that is sure to unite people.

2. Herefordshire Cider: A Toast to Local Flavors

Cider production is closely associated with Herefordshire, and a flourishing cider culture is fostered by the many orchards that dot the countryside. Herefordshire's cider culture is refreshing and varied, with selections ranging from classic still ciders to bubbly variants.

- ★ **Cider Tasting Tours:** Take a cider-tasting tour to discover the cider houses and orchards that make the best cider in Herefordshire. Numerous businesses provide guided tours, which let guests try a variety of ciders and learn about the production process.

- ★ **Perry:** A classic beverage created from fermented pear juice that's worth trying is Perry. Because of its refreshing and fruity flavor, it's a great substitute for apple-based ciders, and many bars include locally made perry on their drink menus.

3. A Rustic Delight: Ploughman's Lunch

A classic British meal, the Ploughman's Lunch captures the goodness and simplicity of Herefordshire's food choices. It is a hearty and filling meal that is often consumed in traditional pubs and usually consists of cheese, bread, pickles, and cold meats.

Chapter 3: Hereford's Countryside Escapes

Like a charming haven from the bustle of the big metropolis, Hereford is tucked away in the center of the United Kingdom. Hereford's surrounding countryside offers a perfect environment for people looking for peace and a chance to reconnect with nature. This section will cover the calm retreats, outdoor pursuits, and lovely parks and gardens that make Hereford a wonderful destination for anybody looking to get away from it all.

Calm Encounters Around Hereford

Herefordshire, a region renowned for its scenic vistas, offers a variety of peaceful havens that invite guests to relax and revitalize. The lodging choices are as varied as the scenery, ranging from luxurious country estates to little bed and breakfasts.

The historic Brinsop Court is a particularly notable retreat. This magnificent manor home, which dates back to the fourteenth century, provides a calm retreat for visitors. The surrounding countryside offers the ideal setting for leisure, and the blend of classic architecture and contemporary conveniences guarantees a delightful stay.

The Kilpeck Inn offers a comfortable haven for individuals who would like to be in a more private location. Tucked away next to the well-known Kilpeck Church, this little inn provides fine dining experiences with locally produced cuisine in addition to cozy lodging.

Outdoor Activities: Mountain Biking, Walking, and Hiking

With so much to do, the surrounding countryside of Hereford is an outdoor enthusiast's dream come true. The main activities that let guests take in the abundant natural splendor include hiking, cycling, and nature walks.

A short drive from Hereford, the Black Mountains offers hikers a challenging environment. Paths bend across valleys and rise to expansive heights that provide stunning views of the surrounding landscape. One well-known hike is the Offa's Dyke Path, which crosses the boundary between Wales and England and offers a unique experience of both the natural world and history.

The many beautiful roads that go through the rural areas of Herefordshire will delight cyclists. For instance, bikers of all skill levels may enjoy a leisurely ride along the Golden Valley Cycle Route, which winds past charming towns and along meadows. Inhale the clean air as you ride past undulating hills and through orchards, losing yourself in the peace of the rural landscape.

A peaceful way to discover the local wildlife and flowers is to go on a nature walk. A short drive from Hereford is Queenswood Country Park, which has an extensive system of well-kept pathways winding through historic forests. The park is home to a wide range of bird species, which will thrill birdwatchers. Those who prefer isolation may discover quiet areas along the beautiful lakeside.

Parks and Gardens for Relaxation

Herefordshire's well-manicured gardens and parks provide witness to the county's dedication to protecting its natural beauty. These beautiful havens provide a home for rest in addition to being a visual feast.

Berrington Hall, a National Trust property, has breathtaking Georgian architecture and is encircled by beautifully designed grounds designed by Capability Brown. Wander around the walled garden, gaze at the decorative pool, and enjoy the parkland's beauty. Berrington Hall provides a peaceful haven where nature and history coexist.

The Bishop's Meadow in the center of Hereford provides a more relaxed but no less restorative experience. This large park, crisscrossed by the soft River Wye, is a great place for people to play, have a picnic, or just enjoy the peace of the outdoors. The meadow offers the perfect environment for a relaxed day away from the bustle of the city.

Hampton Court Castle's Waterworks Garden is a must-see for plant enthusiasts who have an affinity for uncommon and unusual species. Surrounded by a magnificent 1,000-acre estate, this 15th-century castle has an elaborate garden with water features, statues, and a wide variety of plant species. With the vivid colors of well-chosen blossoms and the calming sound of running water, strolling through the garden is a sensory feast.

Hereford's rural getaways provide a perfect balance of peace, outdoor activities, and scenic views. Herefordshire offers an enchanted escape, whether you're looking for the comfort of a medieval manor, the excitement of trekking over challenging terrain, or the simple pleasure of jumping through well-kept gardens. Hereford is a destination for those itching to get away from the hustle and bustle of the city because you may embrace a slower pace of life, lose yourself in the peace of nature, and find hidden jewels.

Chapter 4: Art and Culture in Hereford

Both tourists and residents are thrilled with the rich beauty of art and culture that this charming and historically significant city has to offer. This tour of Hereford's art scene takes us through the galleries and museums of the city, through its performance spaces, and into the lively world of neighborhood artisan workshops and studios. Hereford's cultural environment, which ranges from antiquated classics to modern interpretations, is proof of the human spirit's capacity for originality and invention.

Museums and Galleries

Hereford's multitude of galleries and museums bears witness to its dedication to the preservation and exhibition of its cultural history. These establishments provide a wide variety of creative expressions and act as windows into the history, present, and future of the city.

The Mappa Mundi and Chained Library, a rare collection spanning centuries, is housed in the Hereford Cathedral, a magnificent example of Norman architecture. A remarkable window into the minds of those who created the Mappa Mundi, a medieval map of the globe. In contrast, the Chained Library has unique manuscripts and volumes that provide a historical overview of the written word.

The Hereford Museum and Art Gallery offers a carefully chosen selection of paintings, sculptures, and multimedia projects for fans of modern art. In this area, local and international artists come together to create a lively conversation between innovation and tradition. Every visit to the museum is certain to be a novel experience in the always-changing realm of contemporary art, thanks to its rotating displays.

The Old House Museum, located in the center of the city, allows guests to go back in time. This carefully renovated Jacobean structure provides an insight into 17th-century household life. The interactive displays and period-appropriate furniture of the museum provide a multisensory exploration of Hereford's past.

Locations for Performing Arts

Hereford's cultural life is alive and well and goes beyond dull displays to include captivating live events. From classical concerts to cutting-edge contemporary plays, the city's performing arts facilities provide a wide range of experiences.

Located in the center of Hereford, The Courtyard is a contemporary arts facility that serves as a cultural center that presents a range of events. The Courtyard offers events that appeal to a wide range of creative inclinations, including live music, film screenings, dance performances, and theatrical shows. Because of the venue's dedication to accessibility and diversity, everyone can enjoy the arts together.

The Hereford Cathedral is not just a stunning piece of architecture but also a magical place to see choir and concert performances if you like classical music. The cathedral's acoustics improve the listening experience by letting guests fully immerse themselves in the enduring beauty of vocal harmonies and orchestral masterpieces.

Local Studios and Workshops for Artists

The local artisan businesses and studios that dot the cityscape are where Hereford's creative heart pulses powerfully, beyond the formal walls of galleries and museums. These areas encourage a feeling of community among fans and artists alike while acting as creative incubators.

In a serene location in the lovely Herefordshire countryside, the Canwood Gallery presents modern sculpture. Visitors may interact with large-scale sculptures and installations and immerse themselves in the meeting point of art and nature, all while being surrounded by it.

The lively area in the center of Hereford is home to several studios and workshops where regional artists create their works of art. The artisan area, home to avant-garde artists working with new media as well as classic painters and sculptors, is evidence of Hereford's dedication to developing a varied and welcoming creative community.

A hub for up-and-coming artists is the Hereford College of Arts. Collaboration between instructors and students fosters exploration and creativity. By keeping its doors open to the community, the college fosters a relationship between the audience and the artists by letting the residents see the creative process in action.

The panorama of art in Hereford spans centuries, fusing historical narratives with modern interpretations and the unadulterated inventiveness of the city's workshops and studios. The city's dedication to promoting and supporting the arts is clear, from the sacred halls of the cathedral to the cutting-edge venues in the artisan area. Immersion in the cultural view that

Hereford weaves may be enjoyed by both locals and visitors, promoting a profound awareness of the variety of human emotions. Hereford's creative offerings guarantee a trip through time, history, and the limitless regions of creation, regardless of one's level of expertise.

Chapter 5: Shopping in Hereford

Rich in culture and history, Hereford entices shoppers as well as those who like taking tours of its architectural wonders and creative creations. This section highlights Hereford's varied retail scene, which includes everything from the upscale stores lining its cobblestone streets to the lively farmer's markets and locally made goods that highlight the area's artisanal skills. Hereford offers a wide range of shopping options to suit every taste and inclination, whether you're looking for the newest styles in fashion, locally produced food, or distinctive gifts.

High Street Stores and Boutiques

Hereford's old main streets are its beating heart, offering a mix of well-known retailers and quaint businesses to the discerning consumer. The main retail area of the city, High Town, is a busy center that combines contemporary convenience with a hint of vintage elegance.

The High Town stores cater to fashion fans with a wide variety of styles, from quirky independent brands to high-end designer clothes. These streets are home to a wide variety of stores, including Grace's Boutique, which is well-known for its carefully chosen selection of stylish, modern apparel. High Town is a refuge for anyone looking to add distinctive and fashionable pieces to their wardrobes since shoppers may discover a combination of local and worldwide fashion trends.

Hereford's high streets are home to specialist stores that cater to a wide range of interests in addition to apparel. The Hereford bookstore is a renowned independent bookstore where book enthusiasts may get lost in the stacks. The Chocolate Deli, on the other hand, entices those with a sweet craving by serving artisanal chocolates and confections that highlight the region's delectable cuisine.

High Town's Independent Quarter is a hidden gem for one-of-a-kind and handcrafted goods.

With unique home décor at Booth House Gallery and handcrafted jewelry at Silver Spoon Jewellery, the Independent Quarter has a certain character that sets it apart from other popular retail areas. For those looking for unique objects that capture the rich cultural fabric of Hereford, it's a refuge.

Local Crafts and Farmer's Markets

Visit the farmer's markets and local crafts scene to get a sense of Herefordshire's agricultural riches and to get a peek at the artisanal tradition of the area. These lively areas promote sustainability and a sense of community by providing a direct line of communication between producers and customers.

Regularly hosted in High Town, the Herefordshire Farmer's Market turns the city center into a busy bazaar full of homemade crafts and fresh food. The best of the area is showcased by nearby farmers and producers, who provide everything from freshly baked bread and gourmet cheeses to juicy meats and crisp apples. Taste the flavors of Herefordshire and interact with the enthusiastic people who make these goods available to the public.

Hereford's craft culture, in addition to the farmer's markets, lends a genuine touch to the shopping experience. Market towns like Weobley and Pembridge are part of the Black and White Village Trail, which is home to a wealth of enterprises and galleries. Here, guests may see traditional artists at work as they create everything from elaborately carved wooden sculptures to handcrafted fabrics and ceramics.

Located in the center of High Town, the architecturally stunning Butter Market is home to a diverse range of independent vendors selling local goods and handcrafted crafts. Herefordshire's creative and culinary abilities are shown in the Butter Market, which offers a variety of locally derived products like as hand-knit scarves, distinctive crockery, honey, and preserves.

Souvenirs to Take Home

Without bringing a little bit of Hereford's personality and charm home, a trip there wouldn't be complete. Herefordshire's soul may be captured in the variety of souvenirs available from the city's varied retail scene.

If you're looking for some tasty keepsakes, try a jar of Herefordshire cider chutney or any of the cheeses offered by Monkland Cheese Dairy. In addition to demonstrating the agricultural prowess of the area, these delectable treats also serve as thoughtful presents that highlight Hereford's rich culinary history.

At The Great British Florist, where locally produced flowers are fashioned into exquisite bouquets and arrangements, craft experts may peruse the handmade treasures. These flower arrangements, which draw inspiration from Herefordshire's natural beauty, serve as a beautiful memento of the area's stunning scenery.

The Hereford Bull, the city's distinctive emblem, is embossed on a variety of souvenirs, from keychains to mugs, for a touch of history. These objects are physical reminders of the significance of cattle rearing in the area and of Hereford's rich agricultural past.

Hereford's retail sector offers a wide range of experiences for all kinds of shoppers, blending heritage and contemporary in a harmonic way. Hereford offers a retail paradise for all tastes, whether you're shopping for the newest styles on the high streets, local products at farmer's markets, or distinctive mementos that capture the essence of the city. Through meandering around cobbled lanes, browsing individual shops, and interacting with regional craftspeople, tourists not only purchase material goods but also get fully immersed in Herefordshire's diverse cultural fabric.

Chapter 6: Accommodations in Hereford

Hereford, which is tucked away in the stunning scenery of Herefordshire, has a wide variety of lodging options to meet the various requirements and tastes of its guests. The city makes sure that every stay is not only pleasant but also a reflection of the warmth of the area, offering everything from quaint inns and historic hotels to warm bed and breakfasts. We examine the many lodging alternatives in Hereford in this in-depth guide, emphasizing choices for a range of price points and providing helpful booking advice for a flawless stay.

Hotels, Inns, and Bed & Breakfasts

The lodging options in Hereford combine contemporary comfort with a nod to the city's rich past to provide guests with an ideal stay. There are other choices, such as bed & breakfasts, hotels, and inns; each provides a unique experience that makes the trip more enjoyable.

Historic Hotels

Hereford has several historic hotels that are perfect for people seeking a little grandeur and history. These hotels manage to combine contemporary conveniences with stunning architecture. The Green Dragon Hotel, a historic coaching inn with roots dating back to the 16th century, is one such treasure. With its timbered façade and ancient elegance, The Green Dragon Hotel, located in the center of High Town, gives guests, not just opulent lodging but also a window into Hereford's history.

Another architectural wonder is the Castle House Hotel, which is close to the Cathedral. Within a Georgian mansion, this boutique hotel radiates refinement and elegance. A favorite among discriminating tourists, the Castle House Hotel is renowned for its attention to detail, individual service, and the marriage of traditional features with modern conveniences.

Charming Inns

These inns, which are scattered across the countryside and provide a peaceful respite from the hustle and bustle of the city, are a testament to the rural beauty of Herefordshire. Located in the charming town of Kilpeck, the Kilpeck Inn is a prime example. This 18th-century coaching inn has comfortable accommodations, a friendly bar, and a restaurant serving food that is produced nearby. Intimate surroundings and attentive care make the Kilpeck Inn a home away from home for those looking for a tranquil getaway.

The Booth Hall is a historic inn in the center of Hereford that blends contemporary amenities with an ambiance of bygone eras. Constructed in the 17th century, The Booth Hall offers cozy accommodations and a classic bar that acts as a hub for both residents and tourists.

Cozy Bed and Breakfast

Bed and breakfasts may be found all across Hereford for a more individualized and private experience. They provide a cozy setting and an opportunity to interact with local hosts.

The Westbrook Court Bed & Breakfast, set in a converted cider mill, provides a unique blend of rustic charm and contemporary comfort. Surrounded by orchards and gardens, Westbrook Court offers a calm setting for a relaxing stay.

Situated close to the Cathedral, Castle Hill Guest House is an additional charming bed and breakfast that seamlessly blends contemporary conveniences with Victorian style. For visitors looking for a cozy and inviting atmosphere, Castle Hill Guest House is a top choice because of its attentive care and individual touches.

Accommodation Options for Different Budgets

Hereford's lodging options span a broad price range, so guests may choose affordable choices without sacrificing comfort or quality. Hereford offers a variety of options for those looking for luxurious accommodations or more affordable options.

Cost-effective Choices

Hereford has a range of reasonably priced travel alternatives that don't compromise on comfort for price-conscious tourists. The reasonably priced, spotlessly clean rooms of the Premier Inn Hereford City Centre are situated in a convenient location. For those on a tight budget who want to see the city, it's a great option because of its close proximity to High Town and major attractions.

Travelodge Hereford Grafton is an additional affordable choice that provides basic but comfortable lodging. This low-cost motel is conveniently situated next to the River Wye, giving it easy access to both the city center and the surrounding countryside.

Mid-Range Comfort

Mid-range lodging options that provide a variety of facilities and good value for money are an option for those looking for a compromise between price and comfort. Situated on the outskirts of Hereford, the Three Counties Hotel offers well-appointed accommodations, a dining area, and recreational amenities. Its attraction is increased by its closeness to the Wye Valley and the Hereford Racecourse.

The Munstone House is a little hotel with a Georgian flair that offers a peaceful environment without going over budget. This mid-range property, set within acres of grounds, provides a quiet haven only minutes from Hereford's attractions.

Luxurious Getaways

Hereford offers lodgings that redefine luxury and pleasure for individuals with a taste for the finer things in life. Situated in the neighboring hamlet of Ledbury, The Verzon House is a boutique hotel that blends sophisticated interior design with fine food. The Verzon House is a luxurious retreat with specially designed suites and an emphasis on culinary quality.

A private and exclusive event may be held at Dewsall Court, a former rural house transformed into a luxurious venue. For those looking for the ultimate in luxury and privacy, Dewsall Court is a sanctuary with its grand apartments, expansive grounds, and private lake.

Booking Advice and Recommendations

Making the most of the booking process is essential to a smooth and pleasurable visit to Hereford. To maximize your lodging experience, take into account the following advice and suggestions:

1. Book in Advance: There may be a significant demand for lodging in Hereford, especially around holidays or other special occasions. Making reservations in advance guarantees that you'll have more selections and the best deals.

2. Explore Package Deals: Numerous lodging establishments provide packages that include extra benefits like breakfast, tour guides, or spa treatments. Investigating these choices may make your visit more worthwhile.

3. Check Reviews: Travelers' online reviews might provide insightful information about the quality of lodging. A fair analysis of aspects like facilities, cleanliness, and service may be found on websites like TripAdvisor and Google Reviews.

4. Consider Location: Your whole experience might be greatly impacted by the place you choose. It's important to match the location with your interests, whether you choose a more remote getaway in the countryside or a central location for quick access to activities.

5. Establish Contact with Local Hosts: If you choose a guesthouse or bed & breakfast, getting in touch with the hosts will improve your stay. They often provide intimate knowledge about hidden treasures, regional food, and cultural events.

6. **Understand Cancellation Policies:** As life is unpredictable, plans might alter. To prevent any trouble, make sure you are aware of the cancellation regulations of the lodging you have selected.

7. Make Use of Loyalty Programs: If you are a regular visitor to Hereford or want to come back in the future, you may want to join the loyalty programs provided by hotel companies. Points may be accumulated to get offers, free nights, or other benefits.

The variety of lodging options available in Hereford enables guests to customize their stay to suit their interests and financial constraints. Hereford offers a cozy and unforgettable escape, whether you want to stay in a bed & breakfast, a boutique hotel with a historic charm, or a well-known chain hotel with convenience. The lodgings are more than simply a place to stay while exploring the lively streets and serene surroundings of Hereford; they become an essential component of the trip, adding to the experience and fostering lifelong memories.

Chapter 7: Events and Festivals

Hereford is a city rich in culture and heritage, and its calendar is full of festivals and events that take place all year round. The city provides a wide variety of events that attract both residents and tourists, from centuries-old customs to modern festivities. We'll examine the yearly events calendar, feature noteworthy festivals and celebrations, and provide advice on taking part in regional customs that enhance and enrich the Hereford experience in this examination of the vibrant events scene in Hereford.

Annual Events Calendar

The city of Hereford is known for its vibrant community spirit and rich cultural legacy, as seen by its yearly event schedule. The calendar is a colorful view made up of a wide range of activities for all ages and interests, making it a year-round celebration of tradition and life.

Dating back to the 12th century, the May Fair heralds the start of the holiday season. Every year, High Town has a fair that draws people from all over the world with its exciting attractions, vibrant atmosphere, and abundance of vendors selling anything from homemade crafts to traditional candies. The May Fair is a fun way to welcome summer with a charming mix of modern entertainment and old-world charm.

The Hereford Racecourse meetings are held year-round for horse racing lovers by the Herefordshire Racing Club. These occasions provide not only the chance to see thrilling horse racing but also the excitement and companionship of this venerable custom. Surrounded by scenic scenery, the racecourse offers an amazing setting for an exciting day of sports.

Those who like cider celebrate the Hereford Cider Festival, which takes place in late July. The event honors the area's well-known cider-making history by displaying a wide array of regional cider makers and their best beers. Taste a range of ciders, discover the art of cider-making, and enjoy live music performances that enhance the joyous atmosphere for visitors.

The Hereford Food Festival becomes a highlight for foodies as fall approaches. The festival brings together local farmers, chefs, and craftsmen to celebrate the region's excellent and varied food choices, showcasing the finest of Herefordshire's food pleasures. The Hereford Cuisine Festival is a sensory feast, with everything from exquisite cheeses and handcrafted chocolates to gourmet street cuisine.

Celebrated holidays and festivals

Hereford is home to several well-known festivals and celebrations that attract large audiences due to their distinctive themes and cultural importance, in addition to the regular yearly events. The city's image as a vibrant and interesting travel destination for both locals and tourists is enhanced by these events.

The Hereford Arts Festival honors creative expression and creativity and is hosted in a number of locations across the city. The festival offers a venue for both established and up-and-coming artists to promote their abilities by showcasing a wide variety of visual arts, music, theater, and literature. By giving attendees an immersive experience, the Hereford Arts Festival promotes a sense of community and appreciation for the arts.

A gastronomic spectacular that unites independent food producers, chefs, and food enthusiasts is the Hereford Indie Food Festival. The event showcases the culinary expertise of the area by emphasizing the use of sustainably and locally obtained foods. The Indie Food Festival is a sensory extravaganza that includes pop-up restaurants, food markets, and culinary demos in addition to food samples.

The Nozstock Festival of Performing Arts is a very colorful and varied celebration of music. This festival, which takes place on a family-run farm, offers a wide range of live music acts, comedic acts, and engaging seminars. By combining entertainment, community, and innovation, the Nozstock Festival creates an experience that goes beyond ordinary music festivals.

Participating in Local Traditions

Joining in on local customs is a fulfilling and enjoyable way to get immersed in the Hereford spirit. These inherited customs provide a window into the history of the city and give both locals and tourists a sense of identity.

An enduring custom that honors Herefordshire's apple orchards is to attend the yearly Wassail Ceremony. The Wassail, which is often celebrated in January, involves singing, dancing, and bestowing blessings onto the apple trees in order to guarantee a plentiful crop the following year. Participants gather in traditional wassail costumes, and the ceremony often concludes with a communal feast and, of course, the sharing of Herefordshire cider.

The Hereford Mappa Mundi and Chained Library Trust provides guided tours exploring the rich historical heritage of the city for individuals interested in medieval history. The Chained Library, which houses rare manuscripts, and the Mappa Mundi, a medieval map of the globe, provide an engrossing trip through Hereford's intellectual and cultural past. Taking part in these guided excursions provides a more profound comprehension of the city's contribution to knowledge preservation throughout the ages.

With its founding in 1953, the Herefordshire Guild of Craftsmen carries on the heritage of exhibiting and conserving traditional crafts. You may meet knowledgeable craftsmen and see how handmade items are made by going to their events, which include craft fairs and exhibits. Interacting with these artisans not only promotes regional talent but also educates participants about the history of Herefordshire's traditional crafts.

Hereford's lively and dynamic environment is enhanced by its events and festivals, which honor modern ingenuity as well as centuries-old customs. Hereford is a location where culture, community, and celebration come together thanks to its yearly events calendar, famous festivals, and local customs. Every experience adds a layer to the fabric of Hereford's character, whether it's taking in the many tastes of the Hereford Food Festival, watching the thrilling races at the Hereford Racecourse, or learning about the city's medieval past by exploring the Mappa Mundi. Together, locals and guests celebrate, educate, and enjoy the essence of Hereford, adding to the city's dynamic history of customs, culture, and fun celebrations.

Chapter 8: Practical Information

Traveling to Hereford is about more than simply discovering its colorful festivals, rich history, and quaint lodgings; it's also about realizing the little things that add up to a smooth and pleasurable trip. This section covers important travel advice, manners, and traditions in the area, as well as a thorough resource list for emergency contacts and services. Equipped with this knowledge, guests to Hereford may optimize their experience while honoring customs and guaranteeing their security.

Essential Travel Tips

1. Weather and Clothing: Hereford has year-round pleasant weather due to its moderate coastal environment. Checking the weather forecast before packing is advised, since the weather may be unstable. Bring layers to accommodate potential temperature changes, and don't forget waterproof clothing, especially if exploring the countryside.

2. Transportation: Hereford has a well-established bus and rail network. Learn the routes and times for the region, particularly if you want to tour the nearby places.

To make using public transit more convenient, think about getting an Oyster card. Be mindful that left-hand traffic is followed in the UK while driving. Make sure you are conversant with local traffic laws and possess the required paperwork.

3. Payments and Currency: The British Pound Sterling (£) is the currency used in Hereford and the rest of the United Kingdom. Although most places accept credit and debit cards, it's best to have some cash on hand for smaller purchases.

Tell your bank when you will be traveling so there won't be any problems using your card overseas.

4. Language: English is the official language, and the vast majority of residents speak English. However, it's always appreciated when visitors make an effort to learn a few local phrases.

5. Health and Safety: Although Hereford has first-rate medical facilities, it is essential to carry travel insurance that includes medical coverage. Keep any prescriptions you may need on hand, and know where the closest drugstore is.

6. Time Zone: Hereford follows Greenwich Mean Time (GMT) and observes Daylight Saving Time in the summer.

7. Wi-Fi and Connectivity: Wi-Fi is available in the majority of Hereford's lodging options, cafés, and public areas. For uninterrupted access, you should also think about getting a local SIM card or an international data package.

8. Local Festivals and Events: Before making travel plans, consult the schedule of local events. Your experience while in Hereford may be improved by going to events or festivals.

9. Tipping Culture: Tipping is expected for taxi services, pubs, and restaurants. Although not required, leaving a gratuity of around 10% to 15% is appreciated.

Local Customs and Etiquette

1. Greetings and Politeness: In Hereford, being courteous is highly regarded. It's polite to say "hello" or "good morning" to new acquaintances and to use "please" and "thank you" in everyday conversations.

2. Queuing: The British have a reputation for enjoying long lines. Whenever possible, wait patiently for your turn at the back of the line, whether it is at a store, on public transportation, or anywhere busy.

3. Punctuality: Arriving punctually is seen as courteous. Try your best to be on time if you have a reservation or an appointment.

4. Respecting Personal Space: British people place a high value on privacy. When in line or having a chat, try to avoid standing too near to other people.

5. Restaurants for Dining: It is traditional to wait to begin the dinner until everyone has been served. If you require someone's attention, say "Excuse me" and keep your elbows off the table.

6. Pub Culture: British culture revolves around pubs. It's polite to tip the bartender when you enter a pub and wait to be served. When in a group, it's normal to take turns purchasing rounds of drinks.

7. Greetings and Titles: The customary greeting when meeting someone for the first time is a handshake. Unless asked to use their first name, address persons by their titles (Mr., Mrs., Miss).

8. Cultural Sensitivity: Show consideration for the variety of cultures. Hereford is a multicultural town; therefore, it's important to have an open mind and show consideration for those of all origins and religious views.

Emergency Contacts and Services

1. Emergency Services: To get rapid help from emergency services, contact 999.

2. Healthcare Services: In the UK, healthcare services are provided by the NHS (National Health Service). See your neighborhood general practitioner (GP) or the accident and emergency room of the Hereford County Hospital for non-emergency medical concerns.

3. Pharmacies: Local independent pharmacies, Boots, and superdrugs provide over-the-counter drugs and medical advice.

4. Police Stations: The main police station in the city is the Hereford Police Station, which is situated on Bath Street.

5. Lost and Found: If you misplace anything, get in touch with the neighborhood police department or inquire about any places you could have left it.

6. Embassies and Consulates: Get in touch with your nation's diplomatic envoy in London for information on embassy and consulate services.

7. Travel Information: Check with transportation providers for help or get in touch with the Hereford Tourist Information Centre for information pertaining to travel.

8. Utilities and Services: For problems with gas, electricity, water, or telecommunications, get in touch with utility companies or service providers immediately.

Hereford is a city worth experiencing, but getting around town also means enjoying the little things that make the journey go smoothly and pleasantly. With the right travel advice, familiarity with regional traditions and manners, and awareness of emergency contacts and services, tourists may fully immerse themselves in the rich cultural beauty of the city without sacrificing their comfort or safety. To make the most of your stay in this quaint city, be ready for everything from enjoying the local food to attending festivals to just meandering around the old streets.

Chapter 9: Exploring Beyond Hereford

Hereford itself is rich in natural beauty, history, and culture, but the surrounding regions are also fascinating, with charming towns, historical sites, and magical landscapes just waiting to be discovered. We'll go outside of Hereford in this part, emphasizing day excursions to neighboring sites, suggesting routes to take in the gorgeous countryside, and promoting the allure of neighboring towns and villages. The surrounding regions of Hereford beckon with a variety of engaging activities, whether you're looking for breathtaking scenery, fascinating historical sites, or a taste of country life.

Day Trips to Nearby Attractions

1. Wye Valley: The Wye Valley, an Area of Outstanding Natural Beauty (AONB) designation, is a sanctuary for those who like the outdoors. A day excursion along the River Wye's winding paths provides amazing vistas of cliffs, forests, and riverbank towns.

With its charming settlement built on limestone cliffs, Symonds Yat offers expansive views of the surrounding hills and river. Take a leisurely walk by the river or go on a boat excursion to get a different viewpoint.

2. Hay-on-Wye: Nestled on the border between England and Wales, Hay-on-Wye, sometimes known as the "Town of Books," is a literary refuge. Discover its plethora of bookstores, peruse limited edition books, and take in the renowned Hay Festival, which honors literature and the arts.

A touch of history is added to the visit by Hay Castle, the town's medieval fortress. A relaxing afternoon picnic would be ideal against the background of the ruins.

3. The Black Mountains: For those seeking outdoor adventures, the Black Mountains offer an ideal day trip. Hikers may enjoy breathtaking views of the Herefordshire countryside as they go through this historic hill network, which is home to a network of walking paths.

Take a hike to Hay Bluff to get a broad perspective of the borderlands landscape. For those wishing to go away into the bush, this place is a sanctuary due to its peace and natural beauty.

4. Ross-on-Wye: A short drive from Hereford lies the quaint market town of Ross-on-Wye, which is well-known for its Tudor-style buildings and the picturesque River Wye. Explore the local stores, stroll along the riverfront promenade, and pay a visit to the famed St. Mary's Church.

From Prospect Garden's cliffside location, you may enjoy breathtaking views of the river and the surrounding landscape. It's a great place to get some alone time for introspection.

5. Herefordshire Cider Route: Traditional orchards, cider mills, and farm stores may all be explored on a day trip along this popular cider route in Herefordshire.

Visits to cider manufacturers such as Westons and Dunkertons provide a unique perspective on the cider-making process, along with the additional benefit of samples and local varieties for purchase.

Recommended Routes for Exploring the Countryside:

1. Golden Valley Loop: This beautiful route passes through the Golden Valley, which is renowned for its undulating hills and golden-hued scenery. The route begins in Peterchurch, travels via Vowchurch and Dorstone, and ends in Hereford.

Highlights include the timeless splendor of the surrounding landscape and the medieval church in Dorstone.

2. Herefordshire Trail: The Herefordshire Trail is a 150-mile round walking path that is ideal for a more thorough examination. The path passes through a variety of environments, such as meadows, forests, and towns.

Along the walk, the village of Weobley is worth seeing because of its timber-framed structures. Visit St. Peter and St. Paul's Church to learn about the local history or have lunch at the tavern.

3. Black and White Village Trail: Learn about the unique black and white timber-framed houses that define several towns in the area on this self-guided driving tour. Start at Leominster and go to towns including Eardisland, Eardisley, and Pembridge.

Pembridge is especially charming with its old market square. Take your time discovering these medieval communities and soaking in their atmosphere.

4. Scenic Drive in Brecon Beacons: Take a day trip to Wales and explore the Brecon Beacons National Park. Travel through the food-loving town of Abergavenny before arriving at the charming town of Brecon.
Views of reservoirs, waterfalls, and the magnificent peaks of the Brecon Beacons may be seen from the picturesque path. Take a stroll around the ancient Brecon Cathedral or visit the Brecon Beacons Visitor Center.

5. Hereford to Ledbury: This road from Hereford to the charming market village of Ledbury is a quick but enjoyable trip. Walk around the apple orchards and undulating hills, admiring the pastoral charm of the Herefordshire landscape. Ledbury's famous Market House and other timber-framed structures provide a window into the town's history. Take a look around the independent stores, and maybe have a classic cream tea.

Nearby Villages and Towns

1. Ledbury: Exploration of Ledbury, a market town with well-preserved Tudor and Stuart buildings, is encouraged. In the heart of the town stands the ancient Ledbury Market House, which dates back to the 17th century. Reknowned for its medieval stained glass windows, St. Michael and All Angels Church provides a calm area for introspection.

2. Bromyard: This market village, which is tucked away in the Bromyard Downs, has an enduring appeal. The 17th-century market house, local stores, and classic taverns along Bromyard's main thoroughfare. The town's past is revealed in the Bromyard Heritage Centre, and beautiful hikes may be taken in the surrounding countryside.

3. Weobley: Weobley is a classic black-and-white town that takes tourists back in time. Discover the cobblestone roads, pay a visit to the St. Peter and St. Paul parish church, and take in the atmosphere of this charming community. Weobley is a popular destination among photographers and those looking for a peaceful getaway because of its lovely environment.

4. Kington: Kington is a market town with undulating hills all around it, tucked away close to the Welsh border. The Hergest Croft Gardens provide a tranquil haven with their distinctive assortment of trees and plants. A notable peak that towers above the town, Hergest Ridge offers expansive views of the surrounding landscape. Hikers and lovers of the great outdoors frequent this location.

5. Eardisland: Known for its historic bridge and lovely environment, Eardisland is a town on the River Arrow. The community has a feel of a fairytale with its thatched homes and timber-framed structures. Take a leisurely walk by the river, cross the old bridge, and enjoy the peace and quiet of this picture-perfect Herefordshire hamlet.

Conclusion

As we come to the end of our tour of Hereford and the surrounding districts, it is appropriate to consider the many attractions that make this place a fascinating travel destination. Hereford provides a diverse range of experiences for all types of visitors, thanks to its rich history, active cultural scene, and gorgeous surroundings.

The architectural design of the city, which includes the magnificent Hereford Cathedral and the charming Black and White House, is intricately linked with the historical importance of the area. The lively community of talented artisans and artists, the traditional cider-making, and the local crafts all reflect the artisanal legacy of Herefordshire.

The festivals and events that fill Hereford's calendar give the city's identity a vibrant and dynamic touch. Each event adds to the region's unique cultural diversity, whether it is participating in the ancient Wassail Ceremony, savoring delectable cuisine at the Hereford Food Festival, or honoring the arts at the Hereford Arts Festival.

Hereford offers a wide variety of lodging options to suit different tastes, from charming historic hotels that evoke a bygone era to quaint bed & breakfasts that foster a close relationship with the local populace. Visitors may easily explore the city and embrace local traditions and etiquette while being well-prepared for any eventuality, thanks to the useful information offered.

Stepping beyond the city boundaries, Herefordshire is as varied and lovely as its landscape. With their gorgeous scenery, the Wye Valley, the Black Mountains, and the Golden Valley entice visitors with chances for outdoor exploration, leisurely strolls, and quiet times for introspection.

Suggested Reading for Additional Research

The voyage doesn't really stop when we say goodbye to our in-depth investigation of Hereford; rather, it just broadens into the many opportunities that the neighboring places provide. A world of discovery awaits you in Herefordshire, where each bend on the country road reveals a fresh aspect of the surrounding scenery or a historically significant hidden treasure.

To explore the surrounding towns and villages, each with its own personality and tale to tell, think about staying longer. Ledbury's streets beckon you to stroll about with their timber-framed houses and old market house. Nestled among pastoral scenery, Bromyard provides an insight into country life. It is part of the Bromyard Downs. Weobley, a black-and-white hamlet, encourages you to go back in time, while Kington, close to the Welsh border, offers expansive vistas and a tranquil atmosphere.

There are chances to explore literature, go outside, and connect with nature on day excursions to places like Hay-on-Wye, the Black Mountains, and the Wye Valley. The suggested paths for discovering the rural areas provide a blank canvas of undulating hills, orchards, and winding rivers, beckoning you to write your own story among the magnificent vistas.

The Herefordshire Cider Route offers a pleasant excursion into the heart of cider-making country for people who like the excitement of discovery. Along the cider path, interact with regional growers, sample unusual kinds, and listen to the orchards tell their tale.

Farewell to Hereford's Countryside Beauty

Let the memories of old cathedrals, quaint market towns, and the peaceful countryside remain as we say goodbye to Hereford and its picturesque surroundings. You will never forget the views of the countryside that stretch over the city's boundaries. These scenes are shown in vivid tones of verdant meadows, gold slopes, and winding rivers.

Think for a minute about the sounds of cultural events, the fragrances of traditional food, and the warmth of local hospitality. Hereford provided a beauty of soul-stirring experiences, whether you were looking for the peace of gardens and parks, the excitement of horse racing, or the inspiration of art and culture.

Recall the charming bed and breakfasts and inns that served as stopgap residences, the kind hellos in the marketplace squares, and the fascinating stories these historic sites recounted. Hereford has made a lasting impression on your trip narrative with its unique mix of modernity and history, tradition and innovation.

Take the spirit of Hereford with you on your travels; it's a city that encourages you to take it leisurely, enjoy the little things in life, and slow down. Let the memories of this quaint city serve as a source of inspiration and happiness, whether you decide to return for further exploration or to tell others about your time spent in Hereford.

In keeping with the travel theme, may your next travels be full of unexpected discoveries, cross-cultural interactions, and breathtaking views of uncharted territory. May you discover little reminders of Hereford's allure around the globe, serving as a constant reminder of the enchantment that resides at the core of every location you visit. Hereford, a city that beckons with wide arms and promises eternal memories, has said good-bye.

Printed in Great Britain
by Amazon